EXPLORING COUNTRIES

Peru

by Lisa Owings

FORT WORTH LIBRARY

BELLWETHER MEDIA · MINNEAPOLIS, MN

Note to Librarians, Teachers, and Parents:

Blastoff! Readers are carefully developed by literacy experts and combine standards-based content with developmentally appropriate text.

Level 1 provides the most support through repetition of high-frequency words, light text, predictable sentence patterns, and strong visual support.

Level 2 offers early readers a bit more challenge through varied simple sentences, increased text load, and less repetition of high-frequency words.

Level 3 advances early-fluent readers toward fluency through increased text and concept load, less reliance on visuals, longer sentences, and more literary language.

Level 4 builds reading stamina by providing more text per page, increased use of punctuation, greater variation in sentence patterns, and increasingly challenging vocabulary.

Level 5 encourages children to move from "learning to read" to "reading to learn" by providing even more text, varied writing styles, and less familiar topics.

Whichever book is right for your reader, Blastoff! Readers are the perfect books to build confidence and encourage a love of reading that will last a lifetime!

This edition first published in 2012 by Bellwether Media, Inc.

No part of this publication may be reproduced in whole or in part without written permission of the publisher. For information regarding permission, write to Bellwether Media, Inc., Attention: Permissions Department, 5357 Penn Avenue South, Minneapolis, MN 55419.

Library of Congress Cataloging-in-Publication Data
Owings, Lisa.
 Peru / by Lisa Owings.
  p. cm. – (Blastoff! readers: exploring countries)
 Summary: "Developed by literacy experts for students in grades three through seven, this book introduces young readers to the geography and culture of Peru"–Provided by publisher.
 Includes bibliographical references and index.
 ISBN 978-1-60014-621-3 (hardcover : alk. paper)
 1. Peru–Juvenile literature. I. Title.
 F3408.5.O95 20123
 985–dc22   2011005686

Printed in the United States of America, North Mankato, MN.

080111   1187

Contents

Where Is Peru?   4

The Land   6

Cloud Forests   8

Wildlife   10

The People   12

Daily Life   14

Going to School   16

Working   18

Playing   20

Food   22

Holidays   24

Machu Picchu   26

Fast Facts   28

Glossary   30

To Learn More   31

Index   32

Where Is Peru?

Colombia

Ecuador

Peru

Pacific
Ocean

Lima ★

N
W   E
S

Did you know?
Around 8.5 million people live in and around Lima. That is more than one out of every four Peruvians!

Chile →

4

Peru is a country on the western coast of South America. It covers 496,225 square miles (1,285,216 square kilometers). Peru stretches between Ecuador in the north and Chile in the south. Colombia borders Peru to the northeast, and Brazil and Bolivia lie to the east. The Pacific Ocean crashes against the country's western shore. Most cities in Peru lie along the coast. Lima is the largest coastal city and the capital of Peru.

Brazil

Bolivia

Colca River

fun fact

The Colca River cuts into the land of southern Peru. The Colca Canyon is 13,648 feet (4,160 meters) deep, which is more than twice as deep as Arizona's Grand Canyon.

Peru is a land of dry coasts, rugged mountains, and thick jungles. Its coastline features sandy deserts and warm beaches. Farther inland, the land rises into the Andes Mountains. Many peaks in this range rise over 20,000 feet (6,096 meters) high.

The Amazon River flows down from the Andes. It carries more water than any other river in the world. More than 50 other rivers also start in the Andes. Many are **tributaries** of the Amazon. These waters reach **cloud forests** near the base of the mountains. The Amazon **Rain Forest** begins as the land flattens out. It extends to the northern and eastern edges of Peru.

Did you know?

Lake Titicaca lies high in the Andes of both Peru and Bolivia. The Uru people live on this lake. They have built more than 40 islands out of reeds.

Peru's cloud forests stretch between the Andes Mountains and the Amazon Rain Forest. These forests grow low on mountain slopes. The cool air there **condenses** to form clouds and fog. Trees in cloud forests are covered in mosses, **lichens**, and orchids.

Cloud forests are an important part of Peru's **ecosystem**. They provide fresh water for people, plants, and animals when there is no rain. Their plants take moisture from the clouds. Water not used by the plants flows to the towns below.

Did you know?

Many of the plants that thrive in Peru's cloud forests do not need soil to grow. They cling to trees or other plants.

llama

spectacled bear

giant hummingbird

fun fact

The giant hummingbird and giant armadillo make their homes in Peru. They are each the largest of their kind.

The landscape of Peru is home to many different animals. Off the coast, sea lions chase fish, squids, and octopuses. Pelicans, cormorants, and Humboldt penguins often nest on offshore islands. Vicuñas, guanacos, llamas, and alpacas graze on grasses high in the mountains.

Andean
cock-of-the-rock

In cloud forests, Andean cocks-of-the-rock appear as bright flashes of red through the fog. Spectacled bears roam the forest floor. The markings on their faces make them look like they are wearing glasses. In the Amazon Rain Forest, jaguars and ocelots stalk deer, capybaras, and other prey. Monkeys swing through the **canopy**. The trees are filled with colorful birds and insects.

fun fact

English uses a few Quechua words. If you talk about *llamas*, *pumas*, beef *jerky*, or *lima* beans, you are speaking the language of the Inca!

Around 30 million people live in Peru. Just under half of all Peruvians are **Amerindians**. Their **ancestors** have always lived in Peru. Some people still live in the rain forests like their ancestors did for hundreds of years. *Mestizos* are the second-largest group in Peru. Their ancestors are a mixture of Amerindian and Spanish. A small number of Peruvians have European ancestors who came from Spain in the 1500s. Some Japanese, Chinese, and African people also live in Peru. Spanish and Quechua are the country's two official languages. Quechua is the language of the **Inca**, a people who lived in Peru hundreds of years ago. Many Amerindian groups speak their own languages.

Speak Spanish!

English	Spanish	How to say it
hello	hola	OH-lah
good-bye	adios	ah-dee-OHS
yes	sí	SEE
no	no	NOH
please	por favor	POHR fah-VOR
thank you	gracias	GRAH-see-uhs
friend (male)	amigo	ah-MEE-goh
friend (female)	amiga	ah-MEE-gah

Most Peruvians live in houses or apartments in cities. They drive cars through busy streets to get around town. Peruvians take a midday break called *siesta*. Most people come home to eat and rest during this time.

In the countryside, families rise with the sun and go to bed early after a hard day of work. Friends and neighbors are quick to help each other. Most Peruvians in the countryside live in **adobe** houses with dirt floors. Buses and trucks bring people and goods to and from town.

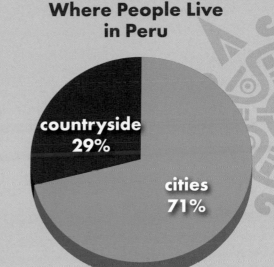

Where People Live in Peru

countryside 29%

cities 71%

Did you know?

Many people in the Amazon Rain Forest hunt or gather food on their own. They make their homes, clothing, and tools with materials from the rain forest.

15

Many children in Peru start preschool when they are 3 years old. All children must be in primary school by age 6. Primary school lasts through sixth grade. Students learn reading, writing, math, science, and social studies. After sixth grade, they move on to five years of secondary school. For the first two years, they continue with basic subjects. Students choose subjects that interest them during the last three years. Just over half of students graduate from secondary school. Of these, around one out of every three is able to attend a college or university in Peru.

Did you know?
Many Peruvian children are unable to attend school. Some live too far in the countryside. Others must help their family earn money.

17

Did you know?

Farmers who live high in the Andes raise herds of llamas and alpacas for their meat and soft wool.

Where People Work in Peru

manufacturing 24%

farming 1%

services 75%

Many people work in Peru's cities. About three out of every four of them have **service jobs**. They work in banks, schools, hospitals, stores, and offices. They also serve the many **tourists** who visit Peru. Factory workers produce steel, **textiles**, food products, cement, and fertilizers.

Miners, fishermen, and farmers work with the **natural resources** of Peru. The countryside is rich with gold, silver, and copper. Miners bring these materials up from underground. Some workers drill for oil. Fishermen cast their nets into the waters off Peru's long coast. They catch anchovies, swordfish, sea bass, tuna, and other seafood. Farmers grow coffee beans, sugarcane, cocoa beans, and cotton for **export**. They also grow fruits, vegetables, and grains.

fun fact

The Inca Trail is the most famous hiking trail in South America. Hikers follow in the footsteps of the Inca, who made the trail over 500 years ago.

Peruvians spend their free time in many ways. Most enjoy playing and watching sports. Soccer and volleyball are especially popular. Peruvians also love to go to the beach. Many swim in the Pacific Ocean or catch big waves on surfboards. Hikers walk through mountains and forests on old, historic trails.

Peruvians also love to relax with family and friends. They enjoy going to movies or staying home to watch dramas called *telenovelas*. Many Peruvians play musical instruments. One popular stringed instrument is the *charango*. Its back is sometimes made of an armadillo's shell!

Did you know?

For many Peruvians, nothing can beat the excitement of a bullfight. Many skilled *toreros*, or bullfighters, perform at the Plaza de Acho bullring in Lima.

Peruvian food varies from region to region. Seafood is popular near the coast. *Seviche* is a traditional dish of raw fish soaked in lime or lemon juice and spiced with peppers. Meat from llamas, alpacas, and guinea pigs is commonly eaten in the Andes. On special occasions, Peruvians in the mountains feast on *pachamanca*. To make this dish, many kinds of meat are cooked together in a dirt pit with hot stones. The rain forest offers a variety of delicious fruits. The *cherimoya* looks like an artichoke but tastes like a sweet tropical fruit. Peruvians enjoy Spanish desserts. A favorite is *arroz con leche*, a rice pudding with cinnamon.

fun fact

Inca Kola is a favorite soft drink throughout Peru. This bright yellow beverage tastes like bubblegum!

cherimoya

arroz con leche

Inti Raymi

Peruvians celebrate many national holidays. To welcome the New Year, Peruvians perform **rituals**. They eat grapes for good luck and carry suitcases for safe travels. On July 28, Peruvians celebrate Independence Day. This is the day when Peru won its freedom from Spain in 1821.

Most Peruvians are **Catholic**. They begin their Christmas celebration on *Nochebuena*, the night before Christmas. On this night, families attend church before returning home to feast and open presents. Easter is observed during *Semana Santa*, or Holy Week. Parades, fireworks, horse races, and bull running bring thousands to the city of Ayacucho during this week.

Semana Santa

Machu Picchu is the most famous site in Peru. The Inca built this ancient city in the 1400s on a narrow ridge between Andes mountain peaks. At an elevation of 7,710 feet (2,350 meters), it is a city in the clouds. The strong walls of Machu Picchu are made of large stones that fit together perfectly. Green **terraces** were built to grow crops and to protect the city from **landslides**.

fun fact

On a hill in Machu Picchu stands a stone pillar called the *Intihuatana*, or the "Hitching Post of the Sun." Its name and shape suggest that it was used to track the sun's movement through the sky.

A five-day hike or a long bus ride brings tourists from the city of Cuzco to the **ruins** of Machu Picchu. No one knows exactly why the city was built. Some people believe Incan kings once lived there. Today, Machu Picchu reminds Peruvians of their roots and the long history of their beautiful country.

Fast Facts About Peru

Peru's Flag

Peru's flag has three vertical stripes. The middle stripe is white and the other two are red. The red symbolizes the blood that was shed to gain independence from Spain. The white represents peace. The middle of the flag features the country's coat of arms. A shield shows a vicuña, a tree, and a basket of gold coins. These images represent Peru's wealth of animals, plants, and minerals. This flag was adopted in 1825.

Official Name: Republic of Peru

Area: 496,225 square miles (1,285,216 square kilometers); Peru is the 20th largest country in the world.

Capital City:	Lima
Important Cities:	Trujillo, Arequipa, Iquitos, Cuzco, Ayacucho
Population:	29,248,943 (July 2011)
Official Languages:	Spanish and Quechua
National Holiday:	Independence Day (July 28)
Religions:	Christian (93.8%), Other (3.3%), None (2.9%)
Major Industries:	farming, fishing, manufacturing, mining, services
Natural Resources:	gold, silver, copper, oil, coal, timber, fish, iron ore
Manufactured Products:	oil, steel, textiles, food products, chemicals, fertilizers
Farm Products:	coffee beans, cocoa beans, sugarcane, cotton, rice, potatoes, corn, grapes, oranges, pineapples, guavas, apples, lemons, pears, mangos, beans, guinea pigs, wool
Unit of Money:	nuevo sol; the nuevo sol is divided into 100 cents.

Glossary

adobe—bricks made of clay and straw that are dried in the sun

Amerindians—peoples originally from North or South America

ancestors—relatives who lived long ago

canopy—a thick covering of leafy branches formed by the tops of trees in a rain forest

Catholic—members of the Roman Catholic Church; Roman Catholics are Christian.

cloud forests—tropical mountain forests that are covered in clouds year-round

condenses—turns from a gas into a liquid, usually because of cooling

ecosystem—a community of plants and animals in their natural environment; all parts of an ecosystem affect each other.

export—to send to another country

Inca—a group of Quechua-speaking people who lived in Peru between the 1100s and 1500s; the Inca were conquered by the Spanish in 1532.

landslides—natural disasters where earth and rock slide down a slope; terraces help protect Machu Picchu from landslides.

lichens—spongy, plantlike organisms that often grow on trees; lichens are a combination of algae and fungus.

natural resources—materials in the earth that are taken out and used to make products or fuel

rain forest—a thick forest that receives a lot of rain

rituals—activities done because of tradition or custom

ruins—the physical remains of a human-made structure

service jobs—jobs that perform tasks for people or businesses

terraces—areas of leveled land; terraces are cut into hillsides and look like steps.

textiles—fabrics or clothes that have been woven or knitted

tourists—people who are visiting a country

tributaries—streams or rivers that flow into larger streams or rivers

To Learn More

AT THE LIBRARY
Croy, Anita. *Peru*. Washington, D.C.: National
Geographic, 2007.

Johnson, Robin, and Bobbie Kalman. *Spotlight on
Peru*. New York, N.Y.: Crabtree Pub., 2008.

Shields, Charles J. *Peru*. Broomall, Pa.: Mason Crest
Publishers, 2009.

ON THE WEB
Learning more about Peru
is as easy as 1, 2, 3.

1. Go to www.factsurfer.com.

2. Enter "Peru" into the search box.

3. Click the "Surf" button and you will see a list of
   related Web sites.

With factsurfer.com, finding more information is just
a click away.

Index

activities, 20, 21

Amazon Rain Forest, 7, 8, 11, 15

Amazon River, 7

Andes Mountains, 6, 7, 8, 18, 23, 26

Ayacucho, 25

capital (see Lima)

cloud forests, 7, 8-9, 11

Colca River, 6

Cuzco, 24, 27

daily life, 14-15

education, 16-17

food, 22-23

holidays, 24-25

housing, 14, 15

Inca, 13, 20, 24, 26, 27

Independence Day, 24

Inti Raymi (Festival of the Sun), 24

landscape, 6-9

languages, 12, 13

Lima, 4, 5, 21

location, 4-5

Machu Picchu, 26-27

peoples, 7, 12, 13

Semana Santa (Holy Week), 25

sports, 20, 21

transportation, 14, 15

wildlife, 10-11

working, 18-19

The images in this book are reproduced through the courtesy of: Herbert Eisengruber, front cover, pp. 26-27; Maisei Raman, front cover (flag), p. 28; Maggie Rosier, pp. 4-5; Kristen Peetz / Alamy, p. 6; South America / Alamy, p. 7; Alexey Stiop / Shutterstock, pp. 8-9; Minden Pictures / Masterfile, pp. 10-11; Juan Martinez, pp. 10 (top), 23 (right), 29 (bill); Matt Hart, p. 10 (middle); Glenn Bartley / Photolibrary, p. 10 (bottom); Bryan Busovicki, pp. 12-13; Eye Ubiquitous / Photolibrary, p. 14; M Reel, p. 15; Michael Doolittle / Alamy, pp. 16-17; Bruce Yuan – Yue Bi PCL / Photolibrary, p. 18; Wildlife GmbH / Alamy, p. 19 (left); Melvyn Longhurst / Alamy, p. 19 (left); Anthony Haigh / Alamy, p. 20; Eitan Abramovich / Getty Images, p. 21; Cris Bouroncle / Getty Images, p. 22; amp Foto Studio, p. 23 (left); Jill Hunter / Alamy, p. 23 (middle); Brent Stirton / Getty Images, p. 24; Oliviero Olivieri / Photolibrary, p. 25; Jarno Gonzalez Zarraonandia, p. 27 (right); Mitrofanov Alexander, p. 29 (coin).